ON BEING IMMORTAL

By
ABBIE GRAHAM

THE WOMANS PRESS

NEW YORK

Other Books by

ABBIE GRAHAM

CEREMONIALS OF COMMON DAYS

VAIN POMP AND GLORY

LADIES IN REVOLT

GRACE DODGE: MERCHANT OF DREAMS

THE GIRLS' CAMP

TIME OFF AND ON

WORKING AT PLAY — IN SUMMER CAMPS

Printing Statement:

Due to the very old age and scarcity of this book,
many of the pages may be hard to read due to the
blurring of the original text, possible missing pages,
missing text and other issues beyond our control.

Because this is such an important and rare work, we
believe it is best to reproduce this book regardless of
its original condition.

Thank you for your understanding.

CONTENTS

IF I HAVE NOTICED ANYTHING REMARKABLE

If I have noticed anything remarkable, it is that the extraordinary lies within the ordinary. Go but a step beneath, beyond, the common experience and you find the uncommon. In the secular, you come upon the sacred. The finite is of a piece with infinity.

Everyone, I believe, desires to take this step. No one is wholly content till he finds his own life related to significance.

I write of the ways in which I have caught glimpses of eternity on a planet suspended here in time.

I DOUBT IF WE ARE BROTHERS
OF THE DUST

From dust we may have come, they say; to dust we may be returning. I do not know.

I am not one to underestimate this dust. If I were choosing my kith and kin, perhaps I might prefer unbroken descent from substantial earth. I should then sense many things beyond all doubting.

My practiced ear would not mistake for rain the crystal tread of snow. Nor should I wonder what hope fills the winged protoplasm of young maples to send them out in spring assault upon a hill by thousands to do battle with uneven chance. I should comprehend a leaf's green business with the sun. I should speak firsthand with chlorophyll. My first duty might then in summer be to know well one birch-lined road or devote myself to one brook bank, its grasses, watercress and mint.

I should know the whole of night, not brief snatches from a city street or summer terrace. No one would say, "It's getting late. We must go in!" Where would in-ness be at that moment when our beloved kin were drawing near from all far corners of the universe?

Yet something in us cannot wholly mingle with

the earth. Perhaps it was an irreparable breach when man stepped out into knowing. Perhaps the earth can never fully take us back, nor we return.

I wonder if the bright leaf with its dual loyalty to earth and air can entirely accept its earth-bound destiny. Is this a joyous shout of homegoing that fills the woods of autumn, or is it red rebellion? Does the snowflake hilariously surrender its brief-patterned beauty to the brook, or is this a protest that I hear as the spring herds the hillside snow down to the endless sea?

I doubt if we are brothers of the dust.

IF IN THE COOL OF AN ETERNAL EVENING

If in the cool of an eternal evening I should eventually come upon the Creator walking in the garden of the immortals, I should wish to be at ease in the revealing moments of that high dusk as we talked gardener to gardener.

I should want to have known how to go proudly in a garden, to have sensed the pleasure of having my word run out to the earth, even though my special portion had been but one small acre of the myriad acreage of the earth.

How could I keep in step with the First Gardener, if I had not been accustomed in spring to say: "Let blue delphinium be there! Let lemon lilies rise bright and golden by the little waters, and sweet alyssum keep the paths in bounds!"

How could I talk at evening with the one Eternal Seedsman if I too had not experienced the daily astonishments hidden in the least of seeds? If I had never stood amazed before the green dichotomy of leaves risen overnight from the seeming unresponsiveness of soil, if I had never watched the blue and orderly march of morning-glories from sun to setting sun, if I had never felt the thirsty soil's release in the time

8

of quietly falling rain—how could I be at home in that first evening?

Nor should I wish to find it necessary to say, "So that is tree-ness there by the river!" I would, I think, be unpleasantly embarrassed not to have had such experience on earth with trees as to know *every tree* when I saw it. I might lack final certainty, for only one by one had I known trees, only wood by wood. Yet there was once at noon an unforgettable yellow maple that I caught unawares making a great melody against the time of winter's silence. On a spring morning there had also been one wood, faintly green, filled with blue sunshine, that said almost all that any wood could say.

I should not wish to feel afraid as the cosmic dark strode in on the heels of evening. Surely in that garden, too, one could stand and watch the neighbors' lights come on, see them swing into customary view, planet by planet. I think I could not gather up seeds, trowel and watering pot, and go in for the night till I had found which planet had been mine.

WHILE AWAITING WORD FROM
THE OPERATING ROOM OF A HOSPITAL

Why do we commit ourselves with such certainty
to life? Why invest wholly in such tenuous estates?
Fragile at the surest are our holdings, hazardous our
tenure, fronting ever on potential loss.

Was not Patroclus slain? Did not David wait in
vain between the city gates for Absalom? Abélard,
was he not forced forever from the life of Héloise?
Was not Niobe bereft, and the Son of Mary cruci-
fied? Milton waked to find the vision of his beloved
Alcestis gone, the day bringing back his night.

We make beautiful a house in which to be left alone
at last.

We clamor to be stripped of peace, to have our
hearts laid waste.

ON THE GOING OF
ONE WHO HAS BEEN GREATLY LOVED

Beloved Earth, we return to thee this dust briefly lent for our delight, hallowed by our love.

Within this little space has the far world been housed. Eternity has been its guest. Holy rituals have here been kept in celebration of the goodness of days.

To keep this last high feast in praise of life, we are come. Here at the moment of its going the light of its mystery falls blindingly upon us. All human experience stands out with poignant clearness. We know ourselves to be a part of a great miracle.

Somehow this bit of dust was awakened to incomparable beauty. Some power filled it, stirred it into tenderness and love, lifted life for us to new levels of good. But now its glory is spent. Whither did its wonder pass in that swift hour?

Thou, O Earth, art enriched forever by this our gift, but let us not the poorer go. Send us not into the spring with empty hearts. Arrest us with the eternal news latent in every created thing. Make us one with rain and winds, with trees and the brotherhood of hills. May we know the solace of fire and all water. Let the bright benediction of sun and moon be upon us, and the fresh glory of forsythia.

THE EXPERIENCE OF GREAT LONELINESS

In winter I have known how lonely a road could be. I have walked in ways that make you certain they have never met a town but have spent their days wandering in and out of gray mesquite brush, in search of destinations long forgotten. I have known rain that has never been acquainted with a roof, returning to earth as it has come, in unbroken solitude. I have stood at night in the streets of a city when fog has clogged the efficient wheels of the smart traffic and erased the brilliant towers one by one, humbling the city to the proportions of any prairie town. I have sometimes been imprisoned within myself by the gray onslaught of doubt and fear.

I have met enough of loneliness to know that it can be a thoroughfare into the whole. The roads that never fully arrived, the rain and fog, even as old an enemy as spiritual incertitude, blot out the lines of one's separate self and merge one with all that has been, all that will ever be.

NO LOVED PERSONS CAN GO FROM US

Neither distance nor death nor misunderstanding can take from us persons who have been loved. Words, gestures, swift insights, little gaieties, tragic hours outlive the brief period of time which houses them. Significant experience is caught up into some ever living medium of the spirit.

All cities that have been shared in common become volumes of quotations. On a momentous day, a person may say inconsequentially, "Let's run into the automat for lunch till the rain is over." One puts a nickel in the slot, and coffee and cream pour out into a cup in constant proportion—coffee and cream, coffee and cream. Or in a many-windowed room that lifts its head proudly in the luminous dusk, a guest turns a moment from the after-dinner talk to look down on the city below, and comments on the extraordinary taste of the city in dinner gowns: "What other city would ever dare to wear that dash of cherry there?" Perhaps others stand in the theater clapping, cheering, then join the stair-descending crowd as one quotes snatches of Richard's farewell to his queen:

"Good sometime queen, . . .
In winter's tedious nights sit by the fire

With good old folks and let them tell thee tales . . .
Tell thou the lamentable tale of me." *

These persons may go to that city long after, alone. The automat may have been removed, the great window of the tall building may stand empty. The theater may have gone the way of theaters. Yet when these come to the street of the automat, they will know. The coffee will pour out in exact proportion, coffee and cream, coffee and cream. The window will remain in the high glowing dusk framing the talk of happy people; and at a certain cross-street Richard will be forever taking last leave of his queen.

Love is that bright amber of the spirit that defies dissolution in the vast waters of unending time.

---

* "King Richard the Second," Act V, Scene I, lines 37-44.

I HAVE TURNED FROM A HOUSE

I have turned from a house in which I have long lived, where I have slept and waked, have gone forth to work and returned again at evening, known festivity and sadness.

I have made the final round of desolate rooms, gathering up electric light bulbs, straggling ivy plants. The floors clatter with emptiness. The windows which have been the spirit of the house stare blankly out into the poplars. Gloom fills the room where dinner guests have gathered. Unfaded oblongs mark the walls where Botticelli's "Spring" has danced, where St. Francis has fed his birds.

Clutching the doorknob for a slow, uprooted moment, I have gone numbly into the street. Yet before the electric bulbs have been screwed into other sockets, before the ivy has reached wanly out to other air, something in me has erased all emptiness. The floors of that house which I have left are now no longer bare. Shelves fill again with the fragrance of linen. Sunlight falls upon a letter I am about to read. A person holds a telegram unopened. A Christmas Eve supper party is talking gaily and being served with cold sliced chicken and fresh home-made bread. "Spring" dances on within a little oblong space. St.

Francis with renewed concern again begins to feed his ever hungry birds.

We cannot, it seems, empty life of living. There is no room for nothingness.

IF I HAVE NOT THOUGHT LOWLY
OF THIS EARTH

If in clear moments I have not thought lowly of this earth I can now make no amends.

I have looked with delight on other planets, marked their swift speed. I have caught a glimpse of Jupiter's nine hurrying moons and the great rings of Saturn. They interest me, yet I do not look on them with envy.

I find that I can love only one planet at a time. One moon seems enough. How could one give allegiance to two moons, or be the confidant of nine? Only this morning, as I came across the pasture meadow from the mailbox, I saw what an emotional responsibility just one moon could be. I happened to turn my eyes for a moment from the letter I was reading, to see how the loosestrife on the knoll was getting on. By chance I caught sight of an apologetic moon apparently ashamed of its unrestrained confessions of the previous evening. It had been so sure but now it hesitated, dawdled irresolutely above the upper firs. Suppose nine moons demanded sympathy of me!

I have, however, wondered from time to time how our fellow planets have fared. Do they have nights there with fragrant winds blowing in from hayfields, cool winds from water? Are there summers that turn too soon to autumn? Does winter come too hastily with snow, duty and committees? Do winters move too tardily to spring? Is there firewood enough, and a long novel of the year?

Has any other planet had capacity to shelter in its whirling waters vast centrifugal love that wrested intelligence from chaos and sent forth a race in search of life that could not have an end?

IN RETURN FOR HOSPITALITY

I had no special appointment with the universe that September noon as I walked through the meadow to the small pond in the hills. My errand could not be called essential, as essentials go. Before I went away for the winter to struggle with uptown traffic and downtown, to run for shuttles, to crowd myself into elevators that could get on without me, I wished to repay this pond for its faithful green hospitality.

Yet it is not too easy to give any small thing to a pond, especially a Vermont pond wholly bent on duty. I could see that it was even now gathering up the waters for its winter ice crop. I put down the bushel basket of dried roots and stood under the maple tree.

What the pond needed, I had decided, was something that it would never get for itself—a necklace of blue iris for the spring. Or was it I who had need of iris, who had never had enough of iris by a water's edge?

I began now to make over the pond in my own image. The excitement of the project took hold of me in earnest. I climbed about the banks, bogged down in springs, crawled through underbrush. All sense of restraint deserted me. I'd not spare iris bulbs.

Nothing can compare to the exhilaration that fills one when duty reinforces delight and delight urges duty to unexpected recklessness. In haste, I spaded up the rich leaf mold, stationed piles of iris around the pond and stooped to plant the first small root.

Something now happened which lay beyond the area of my planning. When my hand touched the earth I felt the universe respond. Between the soil, the root and myself a fresh kinship leaped into being. I became a part of a working trinity that could conquer the cold turmoil of snow and winds so soon to fill this valley, that would bring to life the delicate blueness which slept within these dry roots.

When June came I stood again beneath the maple and knew this must be the pond that I had left. But what had I known of ponds till then, what of iris at the edge of water? Did I say this pond was only bent on duty? Not so. It was completely given to vanity, doubling in its dark waters the spring necklace of delicate blue. One strand of blue would have been enough to cause any pond to lose its head; two were to incite to madness. Where would be our next year's ice crop? Where was anyone sane enough to care?

LET US GIVE THANKS FOR
PLANETARY CARE

Let us give thanks for planetary care:

For a sun and moon that we can count on, for stars that take their station in the evening sky without argument, without any need to be original; for the gray squares of dawn that come unfailingly into bedroom windows arousing to new courage those who watch at bedsides;

For the faithful sequence of the seasons; for the constancy of trees, for their long memories; for poplars that slant upward at the angle poplars always have; for dogwood that maintains its delicate balance, for the way of peach trees standing firmly in new ploughed ground never forgetting to spray the blue sky with the customary pink; for honeysuckle that is so surely honeysuckle that you know it in the darkest night;

For waters that never fail in their devotion to the moon, that move always with deep, sure obedience;

For the steady behavior of elements: for the unvarying affinity of hydrogen for oxygen, of oxygen for nitrogen, for barium's evident decision to be barium;

For the unwavering properties of common salt:

never spectacular, never erratic, but always salt; always conserving; wholly humble, preferring to enhance the flavor of another of earth's commodities;

For the stability of the earth that refuses to be swept off its feet by the climactic ecstacy of northern lights, holding to its course though shaken by wave after wave of dynamic mist, now blue green, now copper green, now pale blue, now magenta.

Let us give thanks for the impartial tenderness of a planet's care.

WE HAVE LET GO OF HOLINESS,
THEY SAY

We have let go of holiness, they say. We do not as a people meet in sacred places to pray a blessing on our bread. We do not bear water in golden ewers and pour it in silver bowls to be blessed by the Lord God of Earth. Nor do we blow a horn and light fires from hill to hill in praise of a young moon that leads a new procession of days. We do not at the season of ingathering take the fruits of goodly trees, branches of palm, boughs of thick trees and willows of the brook and lift them up with rejoicing before the Lord of Heaven.

We cannot sing a song of thanksgiving in the Chicago wheat pit nor do a dance of dividends in Wall Street. Our new houses stand complete with fireplace and running water, laundry chute and letterbox; we have not yet learned, however, the manner of intoning a proper thanks to the creators of cement and plastics.

We do not do these things. We look to science to fortify our bread. Our water supply we trust to chlorination and bacteriological analysis. The banks, the life insurance companies, the enterprising dry cleaners kindly furnish us with calendars by which to pay our rent, to settle bills outstanding.

We are become, they say, a secular people. Science is our shepherd. We are the people of its laboratories, the followers of its statistical curves.

A NEW HOLINESS MAY AWAIT US
If God Were Looking for Office Space

If God were looking for office space today He might find the atmosphere of scientific laboratories congenial to Him. The universal data, the sweeping theses might stimulate Him to ever new creation. He might find Himself at home among the statisticians who deal with masses, among the planning experts. These may be writing a new bible for our time.

The prophets of today may be thundering not in metaphor and parable but in statistical curves, in means and medians. They tell us starkly of low incomes and of high, of the tragic sorrow in the death rates of children of the poor. They tell us of idle men and youth unwanted, of the old who must live in want and fear. Neatly, coldly, they calculate our doom if we turn not again to God.

Revelations may for us now lie in the blueprints of the planners. It may be these who are unrolling for us a new earth and a heaven. Here they show us houses enough for all; there they lay out parks and garden plots. The shore lines could be recovered for the people. The ocean currents might run continental errands of good will. Continents might join with continents. This continent could furnish wheat, that one is best adapted to milk and cheeses or to tin and rubber. So the planners work and seek to interest us in using life for living.

These scientists must surely find grace in the sight of the Lord High God.

In the Breaking of Bread

God lives not, I think, in bread and wine but in the breaking of bread, in the sharing of wine. Bread unbroken does not fortify the heart but bread divided among all who know hunger will sustain the spirit.

There is nothing wrong with communion tables except their length. They accommodate too few. God is not geared to feed the few. He is at his best with multitudes.

PENANCE

A Man Talks in the Diner

I thought at first someone should speak to God about this man from the Heights who kept talking in the diner within earshot of all. He talked of what should be done about *those people in the flats* who now had cars as good as his—soft-cushioned, shining, quiet-moving cars to take them to work down at the steel mills, to take them home again, cars brighter, bigger than their drab houses.

I wondered as I sat at dinner in what bibles, in what constitutions it is written that those who make the cars should not enjoy them, that those who have drab houses should likewise have drab cars.

Thinking thus I looked about in the diner for someone better qualified than I to lead a litany of deliverance from evil. But in that glance I caught sight of the talker. I wondered how this kind of man could ever interest God.

Speed, O God, the Education of the Committee

Speed, O God, the education of the committee. Let it know that black skins can feel a pleasure in the cool night winds of summer, in the buoyance of water; that eyes which look out from dark faces can find delight in the leaping of a campfire's flame, in the grayness of a beech, the greenness of a wood.

How long, O Lord, how long does education of this nature usually take?

On Confronting Mankind in Restaurant Mirrors Among the "Specials for Today"

When I sit at restaurant counters, hopefully searching for luncheon bargains, scanning the magnanimous offers in double-decker sandwiches, dessert and beverage, and confront mankind mirrored among the "Specials for Today," I wonder if these could be of the race that built the Hanging Gardens, that sang of Ilium and Jerusalem, that produced the prophets, that gave birth to Dante, Shakespeare and Cervantes, that evolved the Copernican system and the theory of relativity?

I behold defeated faces, tense faces unreleased by memories of good will, sagging faces ungirded for great deeds, baffled faces uncertain as to whether the eternal news is true.

These soon slip from the mirror, and the faces of other luncheon generations take their places and study hopefully the decorative titles: "Try Our Pie"; "Delicious Hamburgers with Juicy Onions."

Are we, O God, but as the grass that withereth, that today is and tomorrow is not? Are there no songs that must today be sung, no brave deeds demanded by this new day?

For This Dullness

For this dullness that we are willing to accept, forgive us, God!

We sit in rows among the latest kitchenware of this department store to hear an expert demonstrator speak in praise of electric stoves. He asks for a show of hands of those who have seen this stove before, for a show of hands of those who have not seen this stove before. He talks brightly of efficiency. He presses buttons, he gauges heat, he bakes ham. He refers to the courtesy of contributors who gave the ham, the baking pans. . . .

I listened well and I would swear he spoke not of Galvani nor of Volta nor of young Michael Faraday's coming down to London to swing wide the doors opening into the new electrical age.

Forgive us that we can be content with so little truth, so little wonder that we make no demands for miracles!

I STOOD IN FLORENCE BEFORE THE BRONZE DOORS OF LORENZO GHIBERTI

I stood in Florence before the bronze doors which Lorenzo Ghiberti had made for the Baptistery of San Giovanni. I beheld there the story of a people delicately wrought, scene by scene: looked upon the animals of Noah, the lion, the elephant, circling about the ark with eternal grace; saw Abraham kneeling before three guests lately arrived from heaven; witnessed again the courage of a young shepherd boy who had brought low a mighty giant; and faced a prophet too young to be struggling so wearily with a cross.

As I waited thus in reverence before this beauty which had grown out of the spiritual history of never-dying men, I understood why Michelangelo must say: "These doors would grace the entrance to Paradise."

I knew then that it is man's duty to Paradise to produce doors that will give distinction to its entrance, to create such excellence as to make it a great loss if Paradise should not exist.

WHEN ALL IS SAID AND DONE

When all is said and done I should wish to enter heaven with proper grace.

I do not object here on earth to struggling through stormy nights in search of the street number of my host; but I should not wish to have to go from door to door questioning, "Is this heaven?"

Nor shall I, as one suggests, "ask to see God, none of the servants." If I rang the doorbell of heaven and announced, "I've come to see God," and the servant said, "I am God. I am on doorbells on Wednesdays," I should be eternally discomfited to have underestimated heaven, to have measured it by the balance scales of the small planet I had left!

I should want all to know without my telling them that I had come to call on God. One night I saw how it might be done, that is, for me. A dancer was tapping his way across a narrow stage. As he moved between entrance and exit you thought not of coming nor of going. He would step into a little space, empty and uninteresting till now, and awaken it to rhythm and to melody. I did not fear the dance would end. Such beauty could not pass.

The duty of philosophers may be to chart the way

to heaven, the duty of artists to teach us how to make all going an arrival. If then we meet God in this capacity or that, or come unexpectedly on heaven, we can take all excellence in our stride.

ON READING OLD COOK BOOKS

I can look without sadness on the fragile clear-ringing china that outlives the extravagant young hearts of its purchasers. I can accept the longevity of family silver, old dishes and clocks, for these are destined to serve the generations. But how can it be that this cook book outdistanced a woman's three-score years and ten?

Here is her special rule for spice cake at Thanksgiving, there her cheese soufflé for Sunday nights. At the bottom of a yellowed page is her rhubarb and orange conserve. Inserted in the margin are a neighbor's pie crust and another's salmon loaf marked "excellent." On the frayed edges of a crowded sheet is "Grandma Hunter's Cinnamon Cake." Her unfailing proportions that stirred every householder to zealous emulation even to the third and fourth generations are blurred by time. The amount of baking powder, of cinnamon and brown sugar must now be left to the discretion of the new generation.

What records here of pride, of thrift! What material for the poignant memory of children who waited on Saturday morning at oven doors for the "heel" of a fresh loaf of bread, or soft molasses cookies, what smells of dill pickle, of tomatoes simmering on stoves to haunt forever the passersby in those little September streets.

If literature is to be judged by its power to communicate emotion, I would recommend to the literary critics that they consider the old cook books of women who dealt ever in essential daily needs.

YELLOW CHINA UNBOUGHT

In a little shop of a far country I saw a yellow tea set and loved it wholly. From the beginning I knew it to be a hopeless passion. One cannot carry a tea set by hand half way round a world. I turned empty away.

In the interim of years, my reason tells me I did well to go unencumbered from that shop. I have seen all other purchased sets disintegrate before my eyes, cup by cup, pot by pot. Only the yellow tea set remains unnicked, unbroken. Only its brightness glows undimmed.

Yet I wonder sometimes if I had the right to love a thing so much and let it go.

ON TIPPING A WAITRESS UNDULY

I had not asked the day to grant me any special bestowal of grace. Yet as I looked out at life through the three daffodils appointed to spring duty at the luncheon table where I had been seated, I knew that I was about to receive some unmerited dispensation.

I cannot explain how I foresaw the ensuing benefits. Certainly it was not the crowd of Easter shoppers in the great dining room that stirred me and caused my heart to feel strangely warmed. Barricaded behind their respective table sprays of dogwood, apple blossom, iris, they spoke to one another of the glories of their spring ensembles, of windfalls in dinner gowns. Nevertheless the day was to be gracious to me as I had foreseen, encouraging me to make for myself a little island of peace where I might live intensely for a little space in the undisturbed company of daffodils fresh from a garden.

I opened a book. The waitress seeing my vain attempts to peer into its uncut pages offered me the use of a knife. I looked up quickly, wondering by what experiences she had come to see behind other people's eyes but she was already pouring water two tables down. My sparse luncheon of white sliced chicken sandwich and tall pot of coffee arrived. I put the book aside.

Seeing me thus alone, separated from friends, from books, suspended in space, ideas began to hurry to my side. I did not wish to consider them. But one idea would not let me go. It spoke softly: "The celebrations of a year are the spiritual summaries of a people. . . . This Easter that the shoppers unwittingly observe is the celebration of man's most daring desire—the discovery of the kind of life worth living forever. . . ."

But it was not a day for thinking. One by one the ideas left me. Alone again with three daffodils, I lost myself in being. I caught a faint glimpse of unending life, to which I could belong forever.

The noon hour had passed. I rose to go. I wished there might be a way of astonishing God with some symbol of my appreciation. But you cannot tip the Management. It isn't done. Therefore, gathering up my assorted packages for swift departure, I tipped the waitress unduly and left her to deal alone with her astonishments.

I HAVE STOOD IN GRAY RAIN CONTENT

When passing through a countryside by car or train, I can give my attention to conversation, to books, to sleep, except when yellow sweet clover throngs the highways of early summer like pilgrims in golden cowls walking to some high spring feast.

This clover would have been to me as any other roadside plant had it not been for a night of sleeping out in a meadow in time of storm. I had never known a roof so near as that sheltering poncho nor had I ever felt the upholding earth so sure. I waked at dawn to find sweet clover bending over me, chanting lauds with unforgettable grace. I lay still for a moment in that half light listening to the early morning earth. I was swiftly freed from every fear.

As I stepped into that fragrant, steadfast dawn I knew myself to be a person who could sleep out in storms unafraid, who could stand in gray rain content.

THANKS FOR THE AIRMAIL STAMP

For the airmail stamp, so small, so far-reaching, symbol of the invisible lifting power of air currents, symbol of man's long and patient struggle for domination over physical forces, symbol of the instantaneous haste that words demand—and of the heart's swift need.

IN PRAISE OF WOMEN WHO CLEAN
IN THE NIGHT

Let us praise the unseen hands that in the long night hours sweep and scrub and dust the great buildings of the cities, room by room, floor by floor; that create order out of chaos, leave clips in place, papers in alignment, wastebaskets empty of discarded committee lists, outworn ideas; that exchange the stale air of yesterday's telephone calls for the clean, straightforward fragrance of soap.

40

BENEDICTION OF A GOLDEN BIRCH
IN OCTOBER
For One Passing Beneath It

Let this beauty heal the wounds of bitterness, of misunderstanding. Let this far-extending grace restore trust; this joy, enkindled by the everlasting earth, melt the recalcitrance of the heart.

BENEDICTION FOR A LOVED PERSON
By One Entering into Danger

May the memory of our hours together bless you and keep you in beauty and in strength.

BEFORE ST. MICHAEL'S ALTAR

Grant, O God, that we may constantly stand in the presence of the good, its will to do, its purposes to glorify.

BRIEF, O GOD, MAY BE THE FLAME OF OUR INDIVIDUAL LIVES

Brief, O God, may be the flame of our individual lives, but let us not forget that to the kindling of each an ongoing universe has bent itself.

As we move in the vast stream of time, let us shelter each flame from the winds of the night, let us cherish each bright flowering of the aeons. Let no bruised reed be broken, no smoking flax be quenched.

Thou who didst create light out of darkness, teach us to join light to light that we may together make a clear white path for the race of man as it goes forward into the uncharted dark.

CPSIA information can be obtained
at www.ICGtesting.com
Printed in the USA
BVHW031827251119
564779BV00003B/12/P

9 781168 675293